Jean Welles' Reading Music On Your Guitar

A Method That Teaches You How To Read
And Play Notes On The Entire Fretboard!

By

Jean Welles

11664 National Blvd. #275
Los Angeles, CA 90064
Phone - 800-391-5412
WorshipGuitarClass.com

"Now to Him who is able to do far more abundantly beyond all that we ask or think, according to the power that works within us, to Him be the glory in the church and in Christ Jesus to all generations forever and ever. Amen." Eph 3:20-21

CONTENTS

WELCOME LETTER

Dear Student,

Learning to read musical notes will open up a new language for you to explore. This book can help you to learn this language. It can help you to read the international language of music.

The book starts very basic with the parts of the guitar and tuning. Some of the terms are used in the course and I wanted to make sure you knew what and where they were. For example, the bridge of the guitar, etc.

After the brief introductions to the guitar, the rest of the course is focused on helping you to understand and read music. You'll be learning all about music while playing exercises, and some songs and solos along the way.

The book is set up for either an individual student to learn with, or a classroom of two or more. Several of the exercises are written as duets so two students can play them at the same time.

I recommend taking a lesson a week. Try to spend between half an hour to an hour a day playing the exercises. Start with the warm-up left-hand exercise before each session. When you move to a new lesson, continue to review the older ones. If one of the lessons is challenging for you, spend a few weeks on it.

If you would like to see these songs and solos in a DVD or with videos, you can visit ReadingMusicOnYourGuitar.com.

It was a joy for me to prepare this material for you, and I hope it helps you to read this wonderful language of music.

God Bless,
Jean Welles

PS. To keep in touch with us and get guitar playing tips, join our free Newsletter Family at WorshipGuitarClass.com. There is a sign up box there, or you can send an e-mail to subscribe@worshipguitarclass.com

Parts of the Guitar

As a musician, you should know the parts of your instrument. Note in the picture below that the top of the guitar is also called the <u>face</u> or <u>belly</u>. The <u>saddle</u> is the little white piece of bone, ivory, or plastic that the strings rest on. The saddle is located on top of the <u>bridge</u>.

The strings are supported on the <u>nut</u> and <u>saddle</u>. The <u>action</u> of the guitar is the distance from the string to the neck (roughly 1/4 inch). If the action is low, the guitar is easier to play, but if it's too low you'll hear a lot of buzzing. You can change the action by adjusting the height of the saddle. With acoustic steel-string guitars it's best to take them to a music shop to get set up. There is a metal truss rod that can be adjusted.

The <u>rosette</u> is the decoration around the sound hole. On classical guitars, they are little decorations with pieces of inlaid wood. I saw one with tiny flowers, each made with 100 pieces of wood. The rosettes can be very elaborate, or very simple. In acoustic steel-string guitars they are a few plain circles.

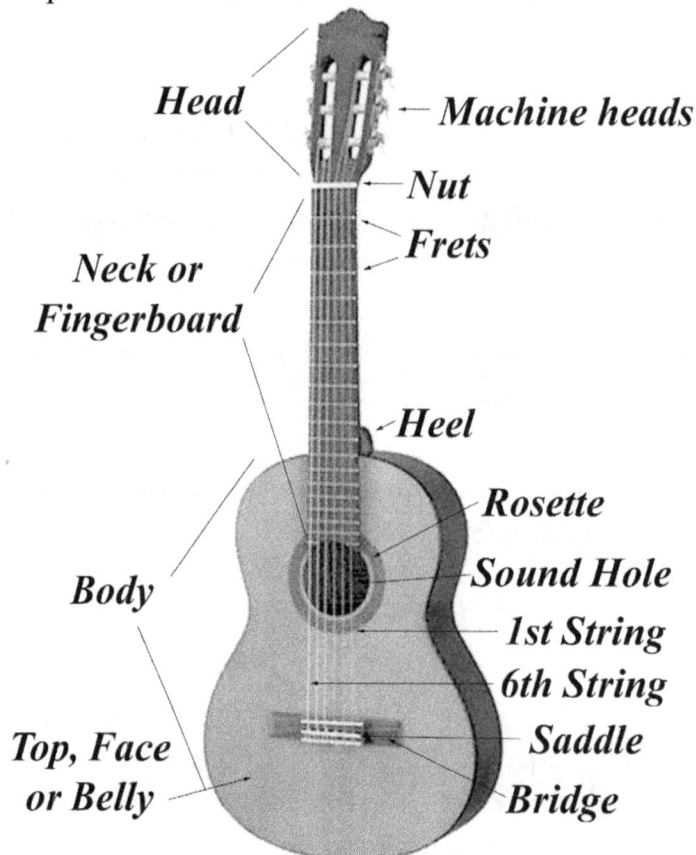

Head — Machine heads — Nut — Frets — Neck or Fingerboard — Heel — Rosette — Sound Hole — 1st String — 6th String — Body — Saddle — Top, Face or Belly — Bridge

How To Tune Your Guitar

Guitars use what is called Tempered Tuning. It's the same tuning as a piano. On fretless instruments, like the violin, a sharp and flat are slightly different notes. Violinists don't hold down the exact same spot like pianists or guitarists.

Did you know the early keyboard players only played in a few keys? It was JS Bach that wrote a whole series of musical pieces for the 'Well-Tempered Clavier'. The tuning is equal for all the notes and our ears compensate for the small difference. Here is how to tune the guitar to itself.

» Tune a Guitar to Itself

The notes of the guitar from the lowest to highest are: E, A, D, G, B, E.

To tune a guitar, you can get the first pitch with a tuning fork, pitch pipe, or simply tune your guitar to itself.

- Tune the 5th string by plucking the note on the 6th string, 5th fret and then matching that with the 5th string open.
- Tune the 4th string by plucking the note on the 5th string, 5th fret and then matching that to the 4th string open.
- Tune the 3rd string by plucking the note on the 4th string, 5th fret and then matching that with the 3rd string open.
- Tune the 2nd string by plucking the note on the 3rd string, 4th fret and then matching that with the 2nd string open.
- Tune the 1st string by plucking the note on the 2nd string, 5th fret and then matching that with the 1st string open.

The diagram below shows what fret to hold down to tune the open string below it. For example, there is a '5' on the 6th string, 5th fret to show that it is the same pitch as the 5th string open.

As you can see, you hold down the 5th fret of the string above the one you are tuning, except for the 2nd string. You hold down the 4th fret of the 3rd string to get the sound of the 2nd string open.

If chord charts are new to you, check out the chart on the next page to understand how to read this chart. Basically, vertical lines represent the strings and horizontal lines represent the frets of a guitar.

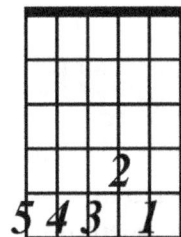

How To Read Chord Charts

As seen in the diagram below, the top line of a chord chart represents the nut of the guitar. The parallel lines below it represent the frets. A chord chart typically shows four frets. The vertical lines represent the strings.

The line on the far left is the 6th string, or the one closest to the ceiling, and the line to the far right is the first string, or the one closest to the floor. Because its pitch is higher, it is called the 'top' string.

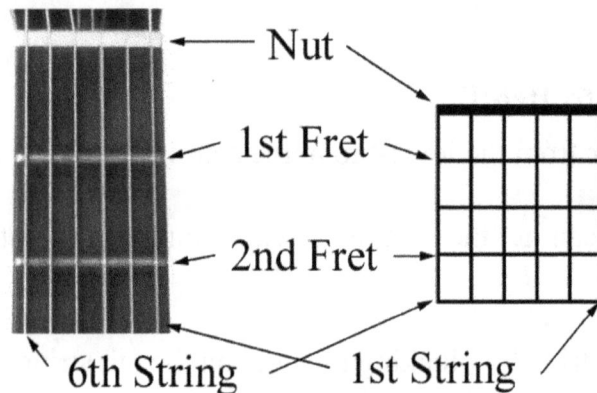

» Guitar Tuners

Automatic guitar tuners are easy to use. Some even play the pitches of each string. Most tuners have a needle which indicates when the string is in tune. When it's in the middle of the gauge, that means the string is tuned.

My current favorite is a Headstock Tuner that clamps to the head of your guitar and tunes it by the vibration of the instrument when each string is plucked. It doesn't matter how noisy the room is. It works by sensing the vibrations of your instrument.

How to Hold a Guitar

When holding a guitar, it's good to have the neck slightly higher than the body. A couple ways to accomplish this is to cross your legs or use a footstool. You can also use a guitar support, like an 'A-frame'. It has suction cups, and elevates the guitar. There are several guitar supports in the marketplace.

Your right arm should rest on top of the body so your forearm can swing easily. With your left hand, place your thumb behind the neck between the 1st & 2nd frets. The thumb should be pretty much behind the second finger. See the picture on the next page.

Names of Fingers

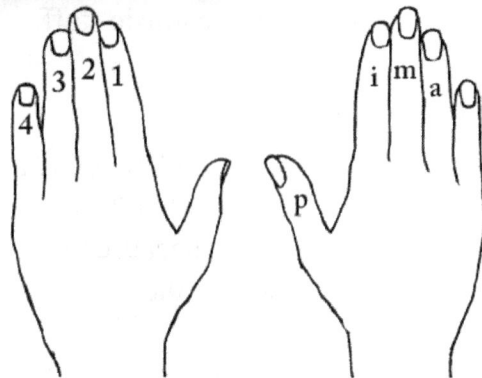

On the guitar, the left-hand fingers are 1, 2, 3, and 4. The index finger is called number 1. I know it's confusing for piano players because they call their thumb number 1. The right-hand uses the letters 'pima'. You will learn more about them in a later lesson.

Rest and Free Strokes

When you are plucking the strings, place the tip of your finger on the string, as in the first picture. A <u>rest</u> stroke is when your finger plucks the string, then lands on the string below. In the second picture the first string was plucked, and the index finger landed on the second string. A <u>free</u> stroke is when the finger follows through in the air, as in the third picture.

A rest stroke is perfect for scales and runs. On page 14 the left-hand exercise is good with rest strokes. Try alternating your fingers between 'i and m'. A free stroke is perfect for playing chords, like the arpeggios on page 18.

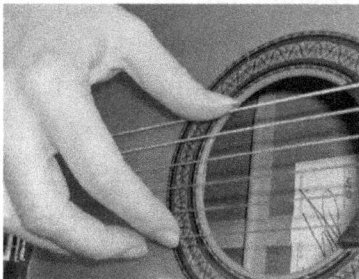
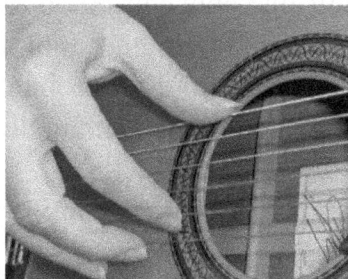
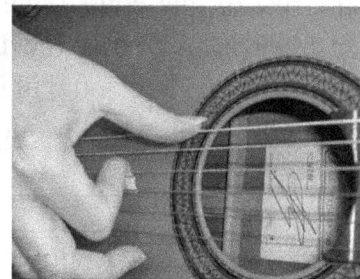

Rest Stroke   Free Stroke

How To Read Music

» Music Staff

Music is basically a combination of rhythm and pitch. In musical notation we use a Music Staff, which is simply 5 lines. The first music notated that we have copies of is called the Gregorian Chant. Gregorian Chants use a graphic notation called neumes. The higher pitched notes were higher on the page and lower pitches lower on the page.

By the 11th century this method of writing music had evolved into using square notation, from which eventually came the modern five-line staff, in the 16th century. Gregorian chant is the root of all Western Music. A music staff is made up of 5 lines, with four spaces. Without a clef sign you won't know the name of the notes on the music staff.

» Clef Signs

The three most common Clef Signs are the Treble Clef, Alto Clef, and Bass Clef. Piano music uses the Treble Clef and Bass Clef. In guitar music we just use the Treble Clef. It's also called the 'G Clef', because there is a little circle around the 2nd line, which is the note 'G'. The other names for the clef signs are 'C Clef' and 'F Clef'.

Some orchestral instruments, like the Viola, use the 'C Clef'. This is a movable clef sign and used in other clefs like the Tenor Clef. In the chart below, you can see where the note called 'Middle C' is located on each music staff with the various clef signs. You can also see why they are called the 'G Clef', 'C Clef', and 'F Clef'. It is very easy to find those particular notes on the three Clef Signs.

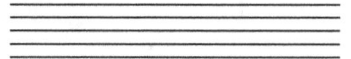

For the rest of this course, we will just concentrate on the Treble Clef, since that is how guitar music is notated. In the diagram below are notes of the first 12 frets of your guitar. By the end of this course you will know these notes. It probably looks daunting at the moment, but soon these notes will be easy for you to play and understand!

The actual pitch of the guitar is one octave lower than written.

10

» Notes on the Music Staff

As you can see below, each line and space of the musical staff represents a note. As you go up the staff, the notes sound higher. There are seven notes in music. It ranges from 'A' to 'G' then starts over again.

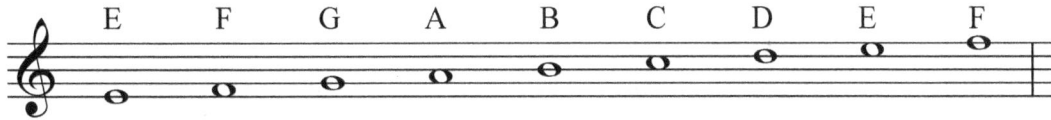

An easy way to learn the notes on the lines is with the phrase 'Every Good Boy Does Fine' or 'Every Good Boy Drinks Fudge.'

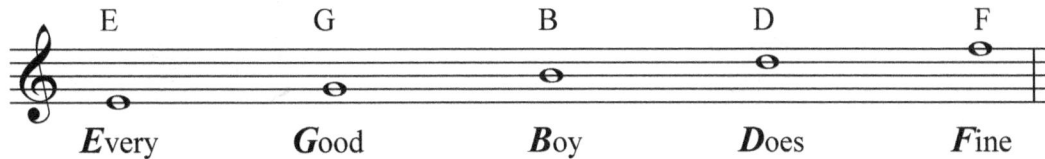

The spaces spell the word F A C E.

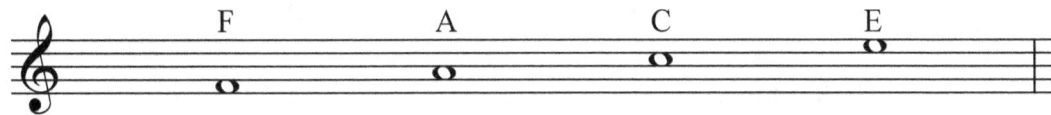

» Parts of a Note

The circle of a note is called the 'note head'. The line is a 'stem', and some notes have 'flags' or 'beams'.

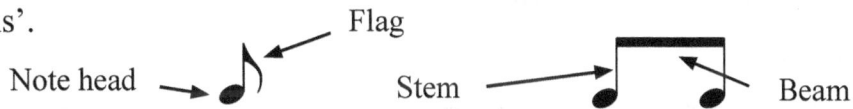

» Rhythm

Music is made of pitch and rhythm. We've covered the names of the notes. Now let's look at note values. Here are the most common note values.

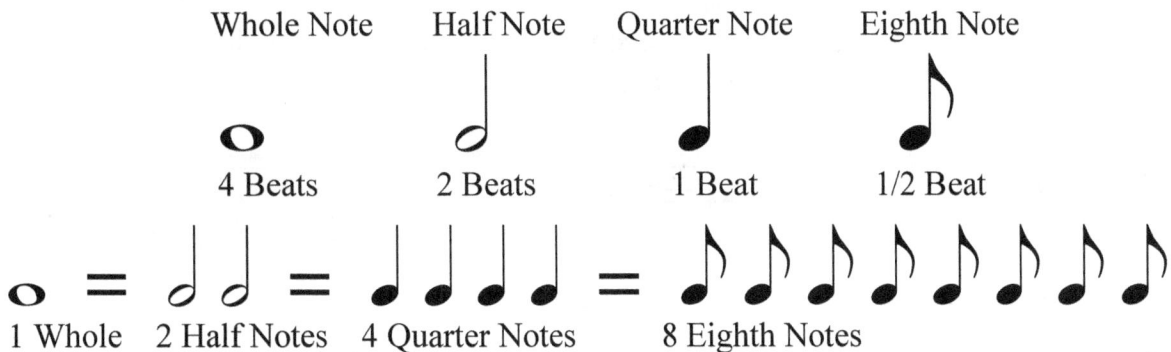

Whole Note	Half Note	Quarter Note	Eighth Note
4 Beats	2 Beats	1 Beat	1/2 Beat

1 Whole   2 Half Notes   4 Quarter Notes   8 Eighth Notes

» Time Signatures

We've covered the names of the notes and written values. You also need to know about time signatures. It's the little numbers you see right after the Clef Sign. The top number represents how many beats in a measure, and the bottom number tells you what note gets one beat.

The most common time signature is 4/4 time. It's also represented by a C which stands for Common Time. The measures are the distance between the little vertical lines on the music staff. The little vertical lines are called bar lines.

Practice Rhythms

Practice clapping theses rhythms. It's a good idea to use a metronome to help you get a good sense of rhythm. You can set it to 76 beats per minute. Each click on the metronome is a quarter note. A whole note gets 4 beats, so you clap once on a metronome click, then let the metronome click 3 more times. Count and clap the following exercises. You don't need your guitar for these.

» Practice Clapping Rhythms

Exercise 1

Exercise 2

The 8th notes in the 7th measure have 2 even claps per metronome click. A measure with 8th notes is counted as '1 and 2 and 3 and 4 and'.

Notes on the Open Strings

The notes on the open strings of your guitar are EADGBE.

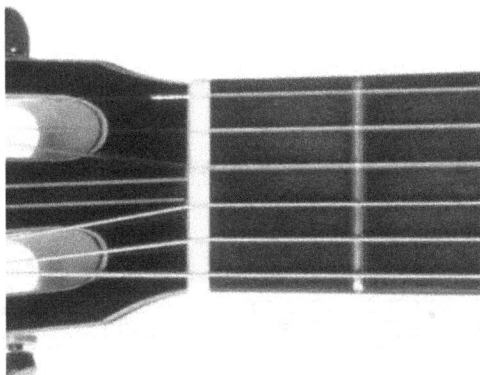

First String ~ E

Second String ~ B

Third String ~ G

Fourth String ~ D

Fifth String ~ A

Sixth String ~ E

It's helpful when playing these notes to say the name of the notes as you play them. You will be learning what they look like on the page and their names. You can either use a finger pick or your fingers to pluck the notes. With fingers, alternate the first 2 fingers. I like to think of the fingers as walking.

» First String - E

Exercise 3

» Second String B

Exercise 4

» Third String G

Exercise 5

» First Three Strings

Exercise 6

Exercise 7

Exercise 8

This one is in 3/4 time, which means there are three beats in a measure. There is also a new note, the dotted half note. A dot after a note means you let a note ring for its full value, plus half its value. A dotted half note gets 3 counts, in 3/4 time, or 3 beats.

Dotted Half Note:

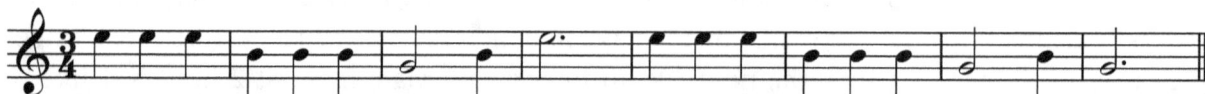

Left-hand Exercise

Exercise 9

We'll finish the first lesson with a good warm-up left-hand exercise. The exercise is done by playing three fingers of your left hand on the first three frets - 123-321. The directions and photos are below. A rest stroke works well for these.

First, try putting the first three fingers down on the first string, first three frets. Without playing, try to keep the palm of your hand parallel to the neck.

Play on the tips of your 2nd & 3rd fingers, but a bit on the side of the 1st finger.

Next, lift up fingers 2 & 3. Try to keep them just above the strings. Play the first string, first fret. Most people tend to place their thumb behind the first finger.

Try to keep your thumb behind the second finger, or 2nd fret. This will help your playing.

Now add the 2nd finger and play that note. Keep holding down the first finger, too. It's much more efficient to keep your fingers down when you are playing scales, riffs, or individual notes on the same string.

Next, add the 3rd finger to the third fret and play the note. Leave your 1st and 2nd fingers on their frets. It's always best to leave your fingers on the guitar when you are playing notes up the string.

After you have played the notes on the first three frets, reverse it and lift each finger up to play the lower note. You pluck the note on the 3rd fret, lift your 3rd finger, play the note on the 2nd fret, lift your 2nd finger and play the note on the 1st fret.

Play the frets - 123, then 321. Try playing the first 3 frets of all 6 strings, beginning with the 1st string. Play the 1st string, 2nd string, 3rd string and so on. This is a little exercise that can help to strengthen your fingers. You can watch a video of this exercise, at the web site - ReadingMusicOnYourGuitar.com.

LESSON 2

Warm-up Exercise with Three Fingers

Start each day with the left-hand exercises that you learned at the end of Lesson 1. It's an excellent one to help you improve your guitar technique. Try to keep your finger close to the fretboard and keep them down on the strings on the way up the neck. Next week we will add the fourth finger.

Notes on the Open Bass Strings

»   Fourth String - D

Exercise 10

'D' is the open fourth string. Remember to play 2 eighth notes on a beat in the 5th and 7th measures.

Exercise 11

This exercise is in 3/4 time. You count to 3 for each measure.

»   Fifth String - A

Exercise 12

Exercise 13

» Sixth String - E

Exercise 14

» First Four Strings

Exercise 15

» First Five Strings

Exercise 16

» All Six Strings

Exercise 17

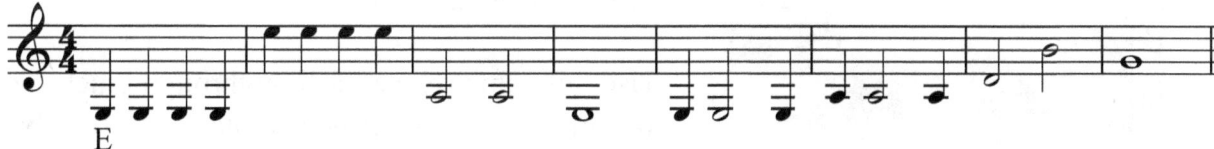

Arpeggios

The rest of the open string exercises are arpeggios. Arpeggios are notes of a chord played ascending or descending. First let's talk about the right-hand position.

» Right-hand Position for Arpeggios

Internationally, guitar music uses the Spanish names for the fingers. The names of the fingers on your right hand are: pulgar (thumb), índice (index), medio (middle), and anular (ring finger). The first letter of each name (p, i, m, a) is the standard references for each of the fingers.

To get the correct position, place your thumb and all of your fingers, except the pinky, on the 3rd string. Place the thumb, p, on top of the string, then i, m, and a underneath the 3rd string.

Looking down, you should see an upside down 'V' between your thumb and fingers.

Move your thumb to the 4th string. Your index finger (i) stays on the 3rd string; middle finger (m) goes to the 2nd string; and your ring finger (a) moves to the 1st string.

Your pinky is not used. It should be in a relaxed position in the air. Keep it slightly bent. It can move with the third finger.

Without moving your thumb, pluck the first three strings with a nice follow-through into the palm of your hand, as shown in the picture.

Use this same relaxed follow-through pluck for the arpeggio exercises below. Start the stroke by planting the index, middle, and third fingers on the first three strings.

Exercise 18

Exercise 19

18

Exercise 20

Exercise 21

Exercise 22

In this exercise the time signature has changed to 6/4 time. The upper number tells you how many beats are in a measure, and the bottom number is what gets one beat. The '4' on the bottom means a quarter notes gets one beat, and the '6' means there are 6 beats in each measure. Count to 6 for each measure.

1 2 3 4 5 6   1 2 3 4 5 6   1 2 3 4 5 6   1 2 3 4 5 6

Exercise 23

In this exercise, you will be plucking all of the fingers at the same time. This is called a Thumb Pluck. Try to follow the diagrams on the previous page. Position your knuckles over the 4th string, and use a nice follow through motion for plucking the strings into the palm of your hand.

It is helpful to keep your hands and shoulders relaxed. It takes energy to pluck the strings, but relax your hand right after plucking the strings. They should fall back naturally.

If you would like to see videos of these lessons, visit ReadingMusicOnYourGuitar.com.

LESSON 3

Warm-up Exercise with Four Fingers

First, try putting all the fingers down on the first string, first four frets. See if you can get the pinky side of your hand as close to the neck as the index finger side.

Play on the tips of your 2nd & 3rd fingers, but a bit on the side of the 1st and 4th fingers. Keep your thumb behind the second fret.

Next, lift up fingers 2, 3, & 4. Try to keep them just above the strings. Play the first string, first fret. Most people tend to place their thumb behind the first finger.

Try to keep your thumb behind the second finger, or 2nd fret. This will help your playing.

Now add the 2nd finger and play that note. As you learned a few lessons ago, leaving your fingers down on the way up a string is most efficient.

Keep fingers 1 & 2 down and add the 3rd finger to the third fret. Next, you add the 4th finger to the fourth fret, as you can see in the top picture on this page.

Play the frets 1234-4321. Play that pattern on all six strings. Try to get a good left-hand position.

The Notes E, F, and G

This week we're going to learn 'E', 'F', and 'G' in several positions on the guitar. As you will see, you can play many of the notes on the guitar in more than one position.

» First Position E, F, and G

Like the warm-up exercise, you can play a separate finger for each note. The little number on exercise 24 are the fingers to use in your left hand. It starts on the open 1st string, 'E', then 'F' is played with your first finger, and 'G' with your third finger.

Leave your fingers down on the fretboard when you are playing higher notes. Leave your first finger on 'F' while you play the 'G'. First position is when your 1st finger is by the 1st fret. Wherever your 1st finger naturally plays, that is the position.

Exercise 24

Exercise 25

Exercise 26

This exercise is written out as a duet. Both parts are using only the notes we have learned and can be played by two students. Although there are two music staffs, this is called one system because the music is played together and read on 'one' line.

Exercise 27

» Fifth Position E, F, and G

Fifth position means that your first finger plays the notes on the 5th fret. Even if you are not using the 1st finger, it's called fifth position. In exercise 28, notice the little circle around the number 2 in the first measure. That means you play that note on the 2nd string.

The dotted line that comes after the circled 2 shows that the entire line is played on the 2nd string. The note 'E' on the 2nd string is on the 5th fret. It is shown in the chart on the previous page.

Exercise 28

» Combining Open and Fifth Position E, F and G

Exercise 29

22

» Ninth Position E, F and G

Exercise 30

Notice that the fingering is exactly the same as the 'E', 'F', and 'G' in the fifth position. This is because the specific relationship between the notes in any position is always the same. The little circle around the number 3 shows that it is played on the 3rd string. The note 'E' on the 3rd string is at the 9th fret.

9th Position

Congratulations! You have now been exposed to these notes up the fretboard. There are many players who start to learn to read music, but seem to only master the first position. After only three lessons, you have been introduced to several of the notes up the fretboard.

Look at that chart again. Is it just beginning to make a little more sense? You can play the same notes in different positions on the guitar. See if you can play and say these notes in the various positions. Next, we are going to add three more notes. Most guitars have a dot at the 5th, 9th, 7th, and 12th frets, which makes them easier to find.

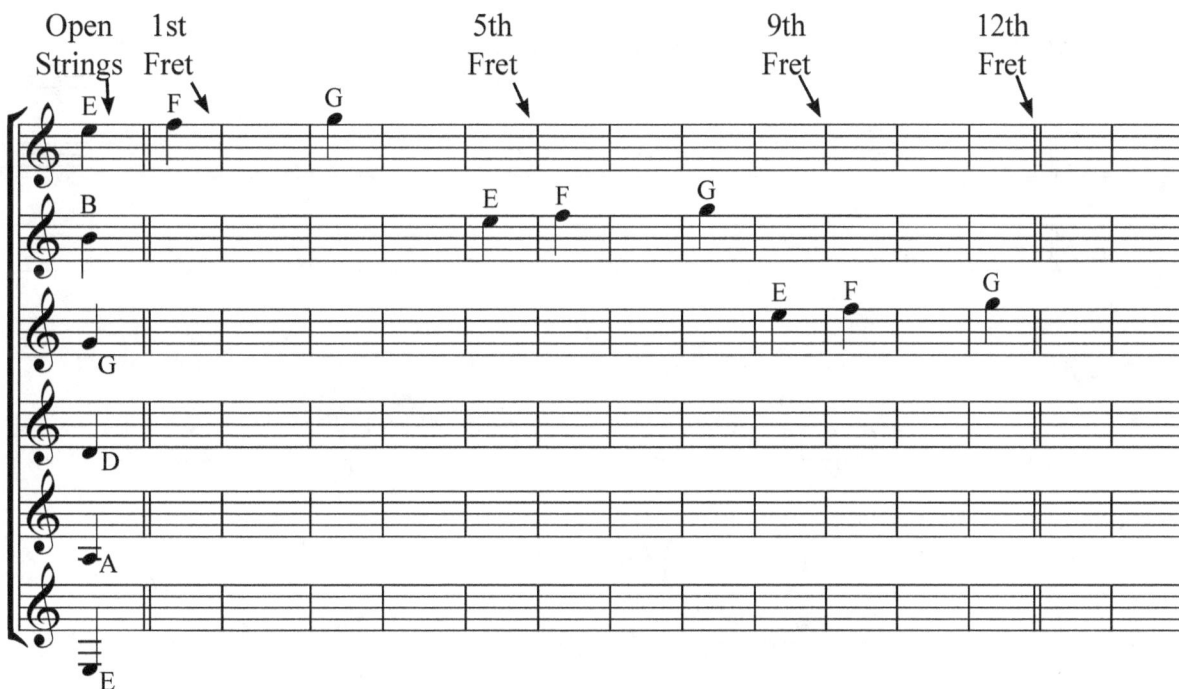

If you would like to see videos of these lessons, visit ReadingMusicOnYourGuitar.com.

LESSON 4

The Notes B, C, and D

Keep playing the left-hand exercise as a warm-up exercise before you start each lesson. There are two more notes for Lesson 4. We will just include the first position notes this week. Next week we will look at 'B', 'C', and 'D' in the other positions. For now, we will only add the 1st and 3rd fret notes on the 2nd string.

Take a look at the chart and play each of the notes. Try playing and saying the name of the note as you play it.

Exercise 31

Exercise 32
Here is another duet for two students to play.

24

O, How I Love Jesus

This song is in 6/8 time. The bottom number tells you what kind of note gets one beat. The '8' stands for an eighth note. Since an 8th note gets one beat, a quarter note would now be held for 2 beats. In lesson 1, you were introduced to the dotted half note.

A dot after any note adds an additional half of the original value. If a quarter note gets 2 counts in 6/8 time, the dotted quarter would get three counts. The last note is a dotted half note. In 6/8 time this gets 6 beats. The half note gets 4 beats and the dotted half note is 4, plus half the value, 2, which equals 6.

The counts are written out in the system to help you visualize where the beats are. Play it in first position.

O   How I   love Je - sus,   O,   how I love Je - sus
1 2 3   4   5   6   1 2 3 4 5 6   1 2 3 4   5   6   1 2 3 4 5 6

O,   how I love Je - sus Be - cause__ He first loved me.

Here is the song again as a guitar duet.

Exercise 33

This exercise uses every note we've learned so far. In the fifth measure, play it in the ninth position, next the fifth, and finally back to first position. The little '0' next to the 'E' tells you it's in first position again, because 'E' is an open string in the first position.

Christmas Song

In the Christmas song below, there are dotted quarter notes. This time the quarter note gets one beat, because the time signature has the number '4' on the bottom. A dotted quarter note has the same value as a quarter plus an eighth note. To count eighth notes you can say 'and' between each beat. The '3' and '+' are underlined to help you see where to play those two notes.

Try to learn, both, where the notes are on the guitar and their names. You may try making flash cards with each of the notes you've learned in these lessons. Quiz yourself on how fast you can play each note and say the name. Play the 'E,' 'F', and 'G' in all three positions.

Remember that the spaces spell F A C E and the lines are Every Good Boy Does Fine. Here are the notes we've covered:

Can you name and play each one? Can you play the last 3 notes in the higher positions? Stay on this lesson until you know these notes. It helps to say and play them for at least 30 minutes a day. Do this and music can become as easy to read for you as a book.

Warm-up Exercise Up The Neck

Remember to start your practice sessions with the warm-up exercise 1234, 4321. This time, instead of playing across the six strings, try playing the pattern up the neck, staying on the first string. Play the first 4 frets, then move your hand up with the first finger on the 2nd fret. Play frets 2 through 5, and so on, up the neck. Move your thumb up, too. To see this, you can view a short video at http://www.worshipguitarclass.com/left-hand.html.

The Notes B, C, and D - More Positions

Look at the chart below. This week we are going to add these notes in other positions. Study the chart below. Try to say these notes and play them.

Learning music is a bit like learning a new language. At first you may just know a few phrases, but the more you use the language, the more those phrases become something you no longer have to think about. You just start speaking.

At this phase, you do have to think about the notes. One of the anchors to help you learn all the notes on the guitar is knowing that the note on the 5th fret is the same as the open string below it, except for the 3rd string. You hold down the 4th fret 'B', which is the same as the open 2nd string 'B'. You will be learning more anchors for memorizing the frets in upcoming lessons.

» Fourth Position B, C, and D

When you're tuning a guitar without a guitar tuner, the fifth fret note is the same as the open string below it, except for the third string. The 4th fret of the 3rd string is the same pitch as the 2nd string open. They are both the note 'B'.

Do you remember the tuning chart from Lesson 1? Here are the actual notes, both in a chord chart and in musical notation.

In later lessons I'll be showing you some other anchors to help you learn all the notes on the guitar.

Exercise 34
This exercise starts in the 4th position, but moves up to the 5th position. In the 6th measure, you see the 1st finger playing 'C', and then a 'B' with a dash right before the number 1. That dash means to slide your 1st finger down to the 'B' and slide it back up to the 'C' in the next measure. Pluck the string each time.

Exercise 35
This exercise moves back and forth between first and fourth position.

28

O, How I Love Jesus - 5th Position

Look how nicely this fits in the 5th position. It is another duet to play.

O, how I love Je - sus, O, how I love Je - sus

O, how I love Je - sus Be - cause__ He first loved me.

Hymn to Joy

This song uses the dotted quarter note. As mentioned in lesson 4, it is easiest to count the beats with 'ands' in between. Say "1 and 2 and 3 and 4 and" for a 4-beat measure. As review, the dotted quarter gets 1 1/2 beats. See the diagram below.

It's in the familiar 'Hymn To Joy' by Beethoven. Play it in the 1st position, 5th position, and 9th position. The only note we have not covered in the upper position is the 'G' at the end of the 3rd system. A system is a line of music written on a music staff. This song is written on four music staffs. It's written on four systems. The 'G' can just be played as the open 3rd string for all three positions. There is a '0' by that note as a reminder.

In first position it starts with the open first string. In fifth position, use your first finger on the 2nd string, 5th fret 'E', to begin the song. Then in ninth position, your first finger will play 'E' on the 3rd string, 9th fret.

Hymn To Joy

Music by Ludwig van Beethoven
From the Ninth Sympony
Words by Henry van Dyke

1st Position

Joy - ful, joy - ful, we a - dore Thee, God of glo - ry Lord of love.

Hearts un - fold like flowers be - fore Thee, Open -ing to the sun a - bove.

Melt the clouds of sin and__ sad - ness Drive the__ dark of doubt a - way.

Giv - er of im - mor - tal glad - ness, Fill us with the light of day.

Hymn To Joy

Music by Ludwig van Beethoven
From the Ninth Sympony

5th Position

Hymn To Joy

Music by Ludwig van Beethoven
From the Ninth Sympony

9th Position

Half Steps Between 'B-C' and 'E-F'

The distance between every fret is call a 'half step.' There are two frets, or a whole step, between all the notes, except between the 'B-C' and the 'E-F'. This is true for all musical instruments. We'll look at this closer next week.

Pianos have black and white keys. It is easy to see the half steps between 'B' and 'C', and also 'E' and 'F'. They don't have a black key between them.

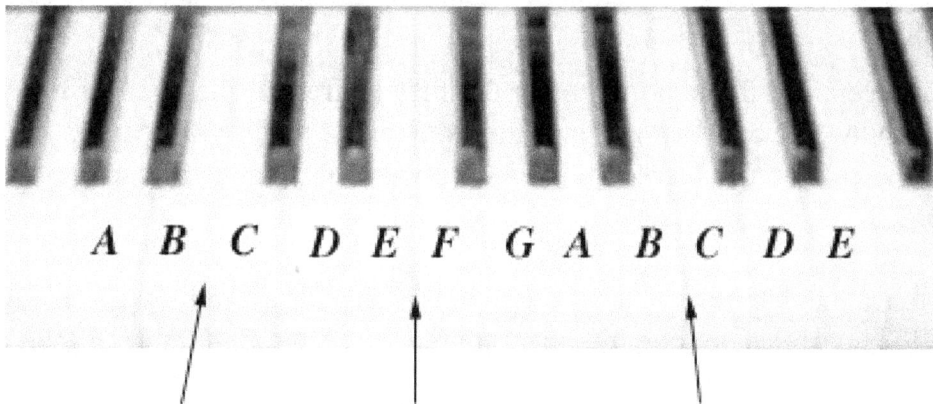

A B C D E F G A B C D E

LESSON 6

Warm-up Exercise Up The Neck

Continue playing the warm-up exercise up the frets. To see this, you can view a short video at http://www.worshipguitarclass.com/left-hand.html.

The Notes G and A In All Positions

This week we are learning two more notes; 'G' and 'A'.

You can now see all of the main notes for the first 12 frets of the third string. Notice that there is an empty fret between most of the notes. Last week you learned that each fret equals half a step. You also learned that the intervals between 'B-C' and the 'E-F' are just one fret apart.

You can confirm that by looking at the chart on this page. Play and say each of these notes. Notice that the notes that are one fret apart are the 'B-C' and 'E-F' notes.

» The Notes On The Third String

Exercise 36
Notice the patterns of these notes as you try them in different positions.

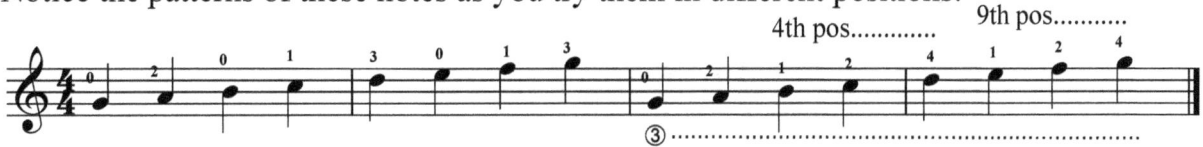

Amazing Grace

What do you do if you want to hold onto a note longer than a measure? Easy... just put the rest of the value of the note into the next measure and 'tie' them together with a curved line. See the ties on the words 'me' and 'see'?

In this famous song, the words 'me' and 'see' are held for 5 counts in a song with only 3 counts per measure. As you can see, there is a dotted half note, which gets 3 counts, tied to a half note in the next measure. Three plus two equals your five counts.

This song introduces a pickup measure. A 'pickup' measure is an incomplete measure that comes at the beginning of a song. In this song the first measure is just 1 count. Music and math are closely related. If there is a pickup measure, the last measure of the song is the difference. One measure, in this song, gets three beats. Since the first measure is just 1 beat, or count, the ending measure has 2 beats, or counts. 1 plus 2 is 3.

Play the melody of the song in 1st, 5th, and 9th position. In first position, the pickup note 'G' is on the open 3rd fret. In fifth position, it is on the 4th string, 5th fret. In ninth position, the pickup note 'G' is found on the 5th string, 10th fret.

Amazing Grace

John Newton

A - maz - ing_ grace! How sweet the sound that saved a_wretch like me!_____ I

once_ was_ lost but now_ I'm_ found, Was blind but_ now I see._____

Amazing Grace played in fifth position is easiest to play by holding down the first 4 strings, with your first finger, at the fifth fret. The '4/6 V' in the music below means to bar 4 of the 6 strings with your first finger.

Amazing Grace

5th Position

John Newton

A - maz - ing_ grace! How sweet the sound that saved a_wretch like me!_____ I

once_ was_ lost but now_ I'm_ found, Was blind but_ now I see._____

It is helpful to remember that the notes on the 12th fret are one octave higher than the open strings. In ninth position, you'll see the octave higher 'A', 'D', and 'G' on the 5th, 4th, and 3rd strings, used in this song. This one is written as a duet for two students.

Amazing Grace

9th Position

John Newton

A - maz - ing_ grace! How sweet the sound that saved a_wretch like me!_____ I

once_ was_ lost but now_ I'm_ found, Was blind but_ now I see._____

Exercise With Two Voices

Exercise 37

This exercise has two voices. The upper voice has the stems going up, and the second voice has the stems going down. Remember, you let the string ring when it is tied to the same note. Be careful not to damp the sound of a note that is supposed to keep ringing.

Bowed instruments, like the violin, or wind instruments, like the flute, can sustain a note for its entire value. The piano and guitar can't make a note louder once it's plucked or struck, but we can continue to let it ring.

Here are the actual notes that you pluck in the above exercise. In this version, the notes are not ringing through. This is included to make sure you understand which notes to actually play. Play the version below, then try the two-voice version again, and see if you can hear the notes continuing to ring for the tied notes.

Exercise 38

35

LESSON 7

Rests

So far, we have looked at various types of notes. There are also rests with the various note values. Here are the notes you have learned, with their equivalent rest symbols. An easy way to remember which is the whole and half note rest is to think of a hat. When the hat is turned upside down, with the rim up, it can hold more. A whole note rest looks like an upside down hat and is a longer rest.

Whole Note = 𝅝 = ▬	Quarter Note = ♩ = 𝄽
Half Note = 𝅗𝅥 = ▬	Eighth Note = ♪ = 𝄾

Exercise 39

You need to actually damp the strings for the rests. A rest means that there is a moment of silence. Here is a little exercise using rests with the bass notes. Stop the string from ringing right on the rest note.

You can stop the string from ringing by putting your thumb back on the string to damp it, by putting the fingers on the string to damp it, or by damping it with the left hand.

Exercise 40

This exercise starts with a pickup measure of two beats. Notice that it ends with two beats in the last measure.

The Notes D, E, and F - In All Positions

Look how nicely the fingerboard notes are filling in. Here are 'D', 'E', and 'F' on the 4th, 5th, and 6th strings.

Exercise 41

This piece uses arpeggios, or broken chords. There are two voices in this song. The notes with the stems up are the top voice and those with the stems down are the bottom voice. Both voices share several of the same notes. The note head shows the longer value.

Although the first note, 'A', is an 8th note for the top voice, it is a half note for the bottom and the note head is shown as an empty circle. You pluck it once, but it rings for 2 counts while the other notes in the top voice are played.

Exercise 42

This little exercise will give you an opportunity to play the 'D-E-F' on the 5th and 6th strings. They alternate with the open 4th string 'D'. The right-hand fingers alternate with the thumb and index finger until the last two measures.

Exercise 43

» Three Voices

Exercise 44

This exercise has three voices all played at the same time. Notice between measure three and four that the notes 'D' and 'A' are the same. You don't need to move your fingers. You can add the third finger to the note 'F' without moving fingers 2 and 4.

Exercise 45

LESSON 8

The Notes A, B, and C - In All Positions

We already talked about the 5th fret being the same note as the string below it, except the 4th fret of the 3rd string. Notice that the 12th fret is one octave higher than the open string. The 6th string, 'E', has an octave higher 'E' at the 12th fret. The 5th string, 'A', has the note 'A' an octave higher at the 12th fret, and so on.

Every fret on the guitar equals half a step in music. Notice the half steps between 'E-F', and between 'B-C'. I don't expect that you have completely mastered all these notes, but you should start seeing the patterns. And I bet you know a lot more about the guitar than just a few weeks ago.

Exercise 46

If you know chords, you will recognize that these are chords. The first is 'Am'. Try to hold the entire chord down at the beginning of the first and third beats.

C Scales

Exercise 47

Here are two 'C' Scales. One is in 1st position and the second scale is in 7th position. Note that the note on the 7th fret is an octave higher than the open string above it. The 6th string open is 'E' and the 5th string, 7th fret is an 'E'. The 5th string open is 'A' and the 4th string, 7th fret is 'A' an octave higher.

I Know That My Redeemer Lives

After you have played the above two 'C' scales you'll be ready to play 'I Know That My Redeemer Lives'. It fits well in the first and 7th positions, like the scales above.

Play the melody of 'I Know That My Redeemer Lives', in both 1st and 7th position. Try to say the names of the notes as you play them to help you remember where they are on the fretboard.

In first position, the first note 'C' is played with your 3rd finger on the 5th string, 3rd fret. In seventh position, the 'C' is played on the 6th string, 8th fret, with your 2nd finger. A position on the guitar is where the first finger naturally falls. Even if you aren't using the first finger, that is how you find the position you are playing on the guitar.

I Know That My Redeemer Lives

Samuel Medley & Johnn Hatton

1st Position

I know that my Re - deem - er___ lives! What com-fort this sweet
He lives to bless me___ with His___ love, He lives to plead for
He lives to grant me___ rich sup - ply, He lives to guide me
He lives to si - lence all my___ fears. He lives to wipe a -
He lives all glo - ry___ to His___ name! He lives, my Je - sus

sen - tence gives! He lives, He lives,. Who___ once___ was___
me a - bove, He lives, my hun - gry___ soul___ to___
with His eye. He lives to com - fort___ me___ when___
way my tears, He lives to calm___ my___ trou - bled___
still the same! O the sweet joy___ this___ sen - tence.

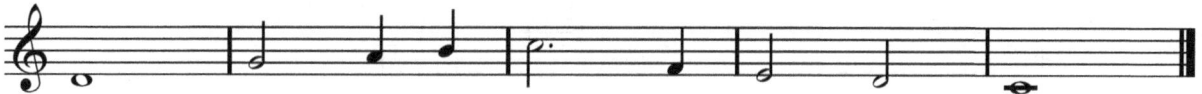

dead He lives, my ev - - er liv - ing Head.
feed. He lives to help in time of need.
faint. He lives to hear my soul's com - plaint.
heart. He lives all bless - ings to im - part.
gives. I know that my Re - deem - er lives!

I Know That My Redeemer Lives

Samuel Medley & Johnn Hatton

7th Position

I know that my Re - deem - er___ lives! What com-fort this sweet

sen - tence gives! He lives, He lives,. Who___ once___ was___

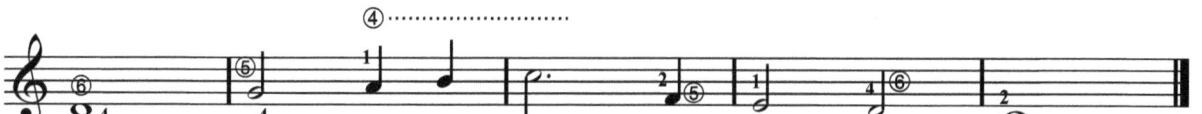

dead He lives, my ev - - er liv - ing Head.

41

The Rest of the Notes

Here is a chart of the rest of the regular notes up to the 12th fret for all of the strings. Play each note on each string and say the notes as you play them. We added the bass notes 'F' and 'G', and the extra notes on the first string.

Notice that the notes on the first string and the notes on the sixth string have the same names. They are exactly two octaves apart. There are 7 main notes in music. They are the letters from 'A' to 'G'. After 'G' is a higher pitched 'A'. Since it is eight notes higher, it is called an octave higher.

I Know That My Redeemer Lives (Duet)

Here is a duet of 'I Know That My Redeemer Lives' for two students. It is written up an octave so you can practice playing some of the higher notes on the first string. The second part includes several chords to help you become accustomed to reading chords, and it also includes the added 'F' and 'G' on the sixth string.

I Know That My Redeemer Lives

Samuel Medley & Johnn Hatton

The Anchors

I want to make sure you understand what I call the 'anchors' for memorizing these notes. Look at the open strings compared to the 12th fret. The 12th fret is an octave higher than the open string. The 5th fret is the same note as the string below, except between the 3rd and 2nd string.

On the next page is a chart showing the relationship of the 7th fret to the open string above it. It's one octave higher than the open string. As you can see, the 5th string, 7th fret 'E' is an octave higher than the 6th string open. The only exception is between the 2nd and 3rd string. The 8th fret 'G' found on the 2nd string is an octave higher than the 3rd string open 'G'.

Knowing the notes on the open strings, you can quickly find any note on the guitar in reference to these anchors. With practice, you can know all the notes without thinking about the anchors, but they sure do help while you are learning the fretboard.

Study by Mauro Giuliani

Here is part of a study by Mauro Giuliani. It's in 2/4 time, which means there are only 2 beats per measure.

Sharps and Flats

We've covered all the regular notes on the first 12 frets of all the strings, but not the sharps and flats. A sharp sign before a note means it is played one fret higher, and a flat sign means the note is played one fret lower. A sharp or flat sign can occur on any note and are called accidentals. A natural sign means the note is back to it's original pitch.

An accidental sign applies to all octaves of the note. It does not apply in the next measure, but it is considered good manner to add a sign when it returns to the original note.

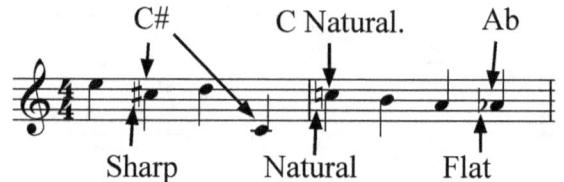

When all of a certain note is sharp or flat, it is written right after the clef sign, and is called a key signature. Different keys have different sharps and flats. So far, we have stayed in the key of 'C' or 'Am'. These keys do not have any sharps or flats.

Here is a key signature with two sharps. 'F' and 'C' must be sharped in every octave for the entire song.

Take My Life and Let It Be Consecrated

Here is a familiar song with one sharp: 'F#'. Notice the # sign on the top line. That means every 'F' in the song is sharped for any octave. Play the song in the 1st position. The 'F#' on the 4th string is the 4th fret. There is an 'F#' in the fourth measure.

Take My Life, and Let It Be Consecrated

Frances R. Havergal
Henri A. C. Malan

Take my life_ and_ let it be   Con - se - crat - ed_ Lord, to_ Thee: Take my hands and_
Take my feet and_ let them be   Swift and beau - ti - ful for Thee;   Take my voice and_
Take my lips_ and_ let them be   Filled with me - sa - ges for Thee;   Take my sil - ver
Take my love, my_ God, I pour   At Thy feet__ its_ treas - ure_store;   Take my - self and

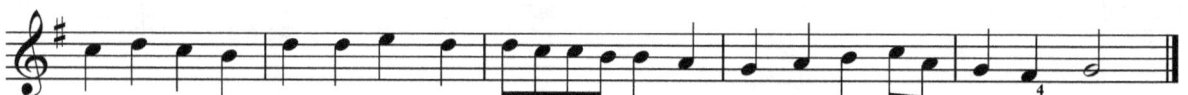

let them move   At the im - pulse of_ Thy love,   At the im - pulse of Thy love.
let me sing_   Al - ways on - ly   for_ my_ King.   Al - ways on - ly__ for my King.
and my gold,   Not a mite would I___ with hold_   Not a mite would I with - hold.
I will be__   Ev - er, on - ly,   all_ for_ Thee_   Ev - er, on - ly,__ all for Thee.

This song also works nicely in 4th position. Play through these notes in the 4th position.

Exercise 48

Now try playing the melody of 'Take My Life, and Let It Be Consecrated' in the fourth position. Play exercise 48 several times, then the song below will be easier.

Take My Life, and Let It Be Consecrated

Frances R. Havergal
Henri A. C. Malan

Knowing how to read notes will open up many new songs for you. When you are leading worship and want to find new songs, you will no longer have to hear a song first. You can simply read it from music books, etc.

For practice, try to read the notes of songs you see in music books. The more you use the skill of reading notes, the easier it will become. With practice, you will soon know the whole fretboard.

A Toy

Here's a fun little Renaissance Lute piece to get you reading more sharps. This song has three sharps. All of the 'F,' 'C', and 'G' notes are sharp. Try playing the scale below to see where the sharps are. After you are familiar with the sharps, try playing 'A Toy.'

Exercise 49

This song comes from the Jane Pickering Lute Book (1615-1645). This song is from the 17th century during the "Golden Age" of Elizabethan and Jacobean lute music. The book is a collection of songs from different composers and some, like this one, are anonymous.

The song starts with three sharps, but in the 2nd system, 2nd measure the 'G' has a natural sign (♮). This means to play the normal 'G' and not 'G#', as it would be in the key signature. You can also see that the last note on the 2nd system says 'G#'. A system is a music staff. This song has 3 systems.

The natural sign is called an 'accidental.' An accidental is an added sharp, flat, or natural sign that is not in the key signature. It applies only to the current measure and applies to every octave of that note.

Although the accidental only lasts for one measure, it's considered good practice to use a courtesy accidental to remind the musician of the regular key. In this case the 'G' is sharped in the measure following the accidental.

A Toy

Jane Pickering's Lute Book

48

LESSON 10

Allegro by Mauro Giuliani

Here is a fun solo to play. There are no sharps or flats in the key signature, but there are lots of 'G#' notes in the solo. This song is built around three chords. You can put the entire chord down at the first of each measure. Remember the arpeggios from lesson 2?

If you know guitar chords, you will recognize that this song is build around 'Am', 'Dm', and 'E7'. Keep the fingers down as much as you can. For example, your second finger can stay on the 3rd string, 2nd fret, 'A' for the first 4 measures. Some of the other fingers will need to move, but that one stays on 'A'.

This solo has repeat signs and a first and second ending. The double bars with two dots are repeat bars. You repeat in the direction of the dots. In the fourth system, 2nd measure, there is a line with the number 1. This is the first ending. At the end of that system, there is a repeat sign with the two dots on the left of the bar.

You, either, need to repeat to the beginning of the piece, or until you see the repeat bar with the dots on the right side of the double bar. In this piece, it is at the beginning of the music. When you play the song the second time, you skip the first ending and go straight to the second ending. Play to the fourth system, 1st measure, then skip down to the fifth system.

Allegro in Am

Mauro Giuliani

Robinson's May

Thomas Robinson was an English Renaissance composer and teacher of the 1600's. This is one of his Renaissance Lute solos and one I've always enjoyed playing. It has three sharps, 'F#', 'C#', and 'G#'.

This solo constantly moves between first and second position. In the last measure of the third system, the last note, 'G', use your pinky. That makes it easier to play the next measure, which is back in first position.

Try to keep the notes ringing for their full value, and remember to keep your fingers down on the way up any of the strings. Hope you enjoy playing this delightful little solo.

Robinson's May

Thomas Robinson

LESSON 11

We Three Kings

This song is in 3/8 time. There are only 3 beats in a measure and an eighth note gets 1 beat. Try playing the melody by itself, then play the instrumental arrangement that is under the song. With two students, you can also play it as a duet.

This is from the 'Jean Welles Worship Guitar Class™ - Christmas Songs and Solos', which is a book and DVD course that also includes the chords and tab for all of the songs. You don't need to use tablature when you can read the notes, so it is not included here. The fermata sign, ⌒, means to hold that beat a little longer.

We Three Kings

Sixteenth Notes and Triplets

An sixteenth note has two flags, or two beams. It is played twice as fast as an eighth note. Is is often counted as '1 e and a 2 e and a', etc. Here's an exercise using sixteenth notes.

Exercise 50

Exercise 51

Exercise 52

A triplet is when you play three notes in the space of two. It is counted as '1 and a 2 and a', etc. It has an even three counts. The main beats do not shift. They should still match up with the metronome.

Exercise 53

Harmonious Blacksmith by Handel

Most of this song is in second position, but it does visit the first and third position. Try to anticipate when you will be shifting to other positions, like from measures 6 to 7. It is good to practice getting the 3rd finger quickly to the 'F#', in measure 7.

The best way to practice a song is to play it very slowly and accurately first. Play it many times and when you are more confident, begin to play it progressively quicker.

You can try playing these songs with a metronome to help you keep an accurate rhythm. Many students play the sections they know fast, but then slow down for parts that are more difficult. Aim for a tempo where you can play the entire piece without slowing down.

Once it's comfortable, aim for a tempo of around 90 beats per minute. This is the tempo for the quarter notes.

Harmonious Blacksmith

Handel (1685-1759)

LESSON 12

Higher Notes

As a refresher, here are the notes in the higher frets of the first couple strings.

Exercise 54

This exercise has four sharps. The sharps are on the notes 'F', 'C', 'G', and 'D'. This exercise is in ninth position.

Exercise 55

This duet is an excerpt from Pachelbel's Canon in D. The top part is in 2nd position until the very last chord.

Away in a Manger

This Christmas song starts in 12th position. The 1st finger is on the high 'E', 1st string, 12th fret. The note underneath 'E' is 'C#' and is on the 2nd string, 14th fret. There are three spots to use a half bar. You hold the top three strings down with your first finger, 1/2 V. They are at the 5th fret and 7th fret, at the end of the first and third music system.

The short slash before many of the fingering numbers means you slide that finger to the next note, and use it as a guide finger. In the third, full measure there is an interesting shift on 'crib for a bed.' The 3rd finger on the lower note, 'F#', moves up 2 frets to play the higher melody note on 'G#'. 'G# and 'E' are both on the 9th fret.

Away In A Manger

A - way in a man ger, no crib for a bed, The lit - tle Lord Je sus laid down His sweet

head. The stars in the sky____ looked down where He lay: The

lit - tle Lord Je - sus, a - sleep on the hay.

Finger Coordination Exercise

Exercise 56

It's good to train your fingers to move independently. This is an exercise I learned from a piano teacher, but it works for guitar players, too. Place your left hand on a table with the fingers slightly curved. Both, your wrist and the tips of your four fingers, should be touching the table.

Lift up the first and third fingers while leaving the second finger and pinky on the table. Bring them back down, and now lift up your second finger and pinky without moving the other two. Tap on the table with the first and third fingers, then the second and fourth fingers, alternately. See how fast you can tap them without raising the other fingers.

55

LESSON 13

Music Road Map Signs

» Repeating measures

We've used some of the 'road map signs' in previous songs. Here are more signs used in music. We've seen repeat signs for entire phrases. There are also repeat signs for 1 and 2 measures.

Repeat the previous measure.

Repeat the previous 2 measures.

» Single note, beat, or chord repeats

The single beat repeat is made with one slash. The first music staff is a shorthand for the 2nd music staff.

1. Shorthand with slashes.

2. Actual notes played.

» 16th Note Repeats

To repeat 16th note patterns, it's two slashes. The first music staff is a shorthand for the 2nd music staff.

1. Shorthand with slashes.

2. Actual notes played.

56

» 32nd Note Repeats

To repeat 32nd note patterns, you need three slashes. The first music staff is a shorthand for the 2nd music staff below it. A 32nd note is twice as fast as an 18th note.

1. Shorthand with slashes.   2. Actual notes played.

» Mixed Note Repeats

Mixed note repeats are the same sign as repeating two measures.

1. Shorthand with slashes.   2. Actual notes played.

To repeat a section of music, there are repeating double bars with 2 dots. The beginning repeat bar has the dots on the right side of the double bars, and the ending repeat bars have the dots located on the left side of the double bars. If there is no beginning repeat bar, you repeat from the beginning of the song.

In the example below, there are three endings. The closed bracket on the first two endings means you go somewhere else. In this case, they both repeat to the top. The open bracket on the 3rd ending means you continue.

Prestissimo by Mauro Giuliani

Mauro Giuliani was considered to be one of the finest guitarists of the early 1800's. This Italian guitarist was also one of the most prolific, and we have hundreds of his works.

The right-hand pattern for most of this piece is 'p m i'. Use a free stroke, so the second voice can continue to ring. A rest stroke would damp the sound. What's interesting about this pattern is the 'p' and 'i' play the same string for most of the piece.

This is an excellent solo for working on your guitar technique. Take it very slow and even, then try to speed it up. Prestissimo means to play as fast as possible, but it is better to play it accurately at a slightly slower speed. See page 54 if you need to remember where the higher notes are located.

Prestissimo

M. Giuliani

Legatos (Hammer-ons and Pull-offs)

On the guitar, legatos are hammer-ons and pull-offs. It is a very smooth and connected sound. For the violin, legatos are played on the same bow stroke. A rapid series of hammer-ons and pull-offs between a single pair of notes is called a trill.

To help you develop this skill, here's a legato exercise. When you are playing the hammer-on stroke, you need to hit the string squarely and with good force. For the pull-offs, you need to pluck the string with the left hand finger. Put all the weight on the finger that is holding down the note you will be pulling off too.

In other words, if you are playing a pull-off from the notes 'D' to 'C#', put the weight on the finger that is holding the 'C#'. This will keep the string steady and help you make a clean pull-off, or descending legato.

The technical names for hammer-ons and pull-offs are ascending and descending legatos.

» Ascending Legato Exercise

You can take this exercise up the entire fretboard. It's on the 3rd string, but can also be played on the other strings.

1 3 1 3 2 4 2 4   1 3 1 3 2 4 2 4.. etc.

» Descending Legato Exercise

Like the ascending legato exercise above, this can be played on all the frets. You might want to practice these exercises with the ascending legatos on the way up, and descending legatos on the way back down the 3rd string.

3 1 3 1 4 2 4 2   3 1 3 1 4 2 4 2.. etc.

Guardame Las Vacas

Here is a lovely Renaissance piece to give you practice with your music reading and with playing legatos. It's a theme with several variations. This means that the underlying chord structure never changes. You can watch a video of this at:
http://www.worshipguitarclass.com/guardame-las-vacas.html

Guardame Las Vacas

Luys de Narvaez-1538

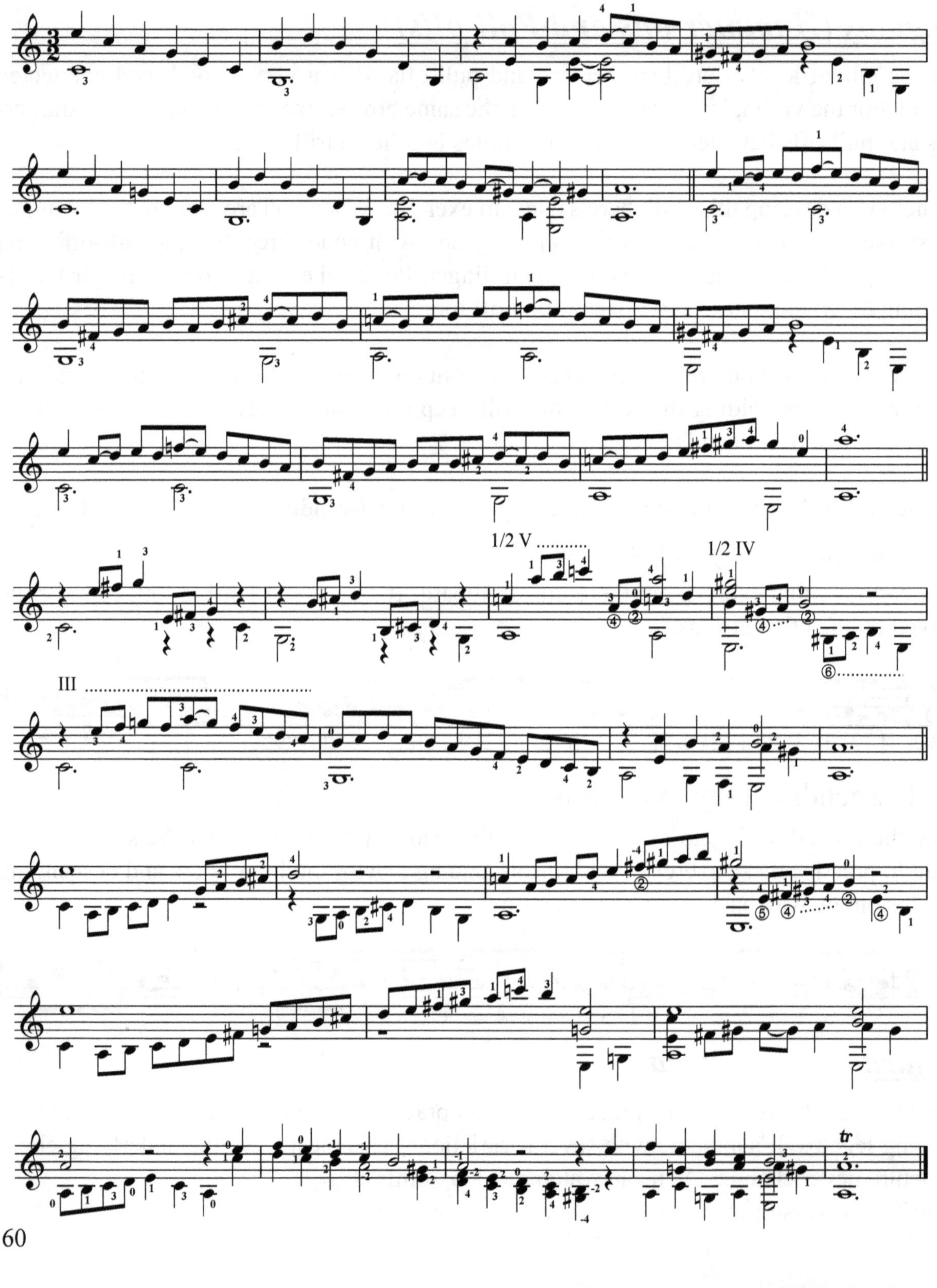

LESSON 15

Tempo Markings

How fast should you play a song? Composers often added tempo markings so musicians knew the tempo that the composer had in mind. Here are some common Italian tempo markings. They range from 'very, very slow' to 'extremely fast'.

Markings	Definitions
Larghissimo	Very, very slow (40 beats per minute, or less)
Largo	Very slow and broad, with dignity (40-60 bpm)
Lent or Lento	Very slow (40-60 bpm)
Larghetto	Rather broadly (60 - 66 bpm)
Grave	Slow and solemn
Adagio	Slow and stately (66 - 76 bpm)
Andante	Walking pace (76 - 108 bpm)
Andante Moderato	A bit faster than andante
Andantino	A little quicker than andante
Moderato	Moderately (101 - 110 bpm)
Allegro moderato	Moderately fast, but less than allegro.
Allegro	Fast and bright. March tempo (120 - 139 bpm)
Vivace	Lively and fast, vivacious quicker than allegro. (140 bpm)
Vivacissimo	Very fast and lively
Presto	Very fast, faster than vivace (168 - 200 bpm)
Prestissimo	Extremely fast (more than 200 bpm)

Etude in Am

This lovely solo by Carcassi is intended to be played 'Allegro', but learn it at a slow tempo before trying to speed it up. Several of the right and left-hand fingerings are written in to help you. Notice the legatos in the piece. For example, at the bottom of page 62 there are several pull-offs.

Keep a relaxed technique and play on the tips of your fingers. Pull-offs are much easier when you play of the tips of the left-hand fingers. It may take several weeks to master this solo. Keep practicing, and you will get it.

Etude in Am

Matteo Carcassi

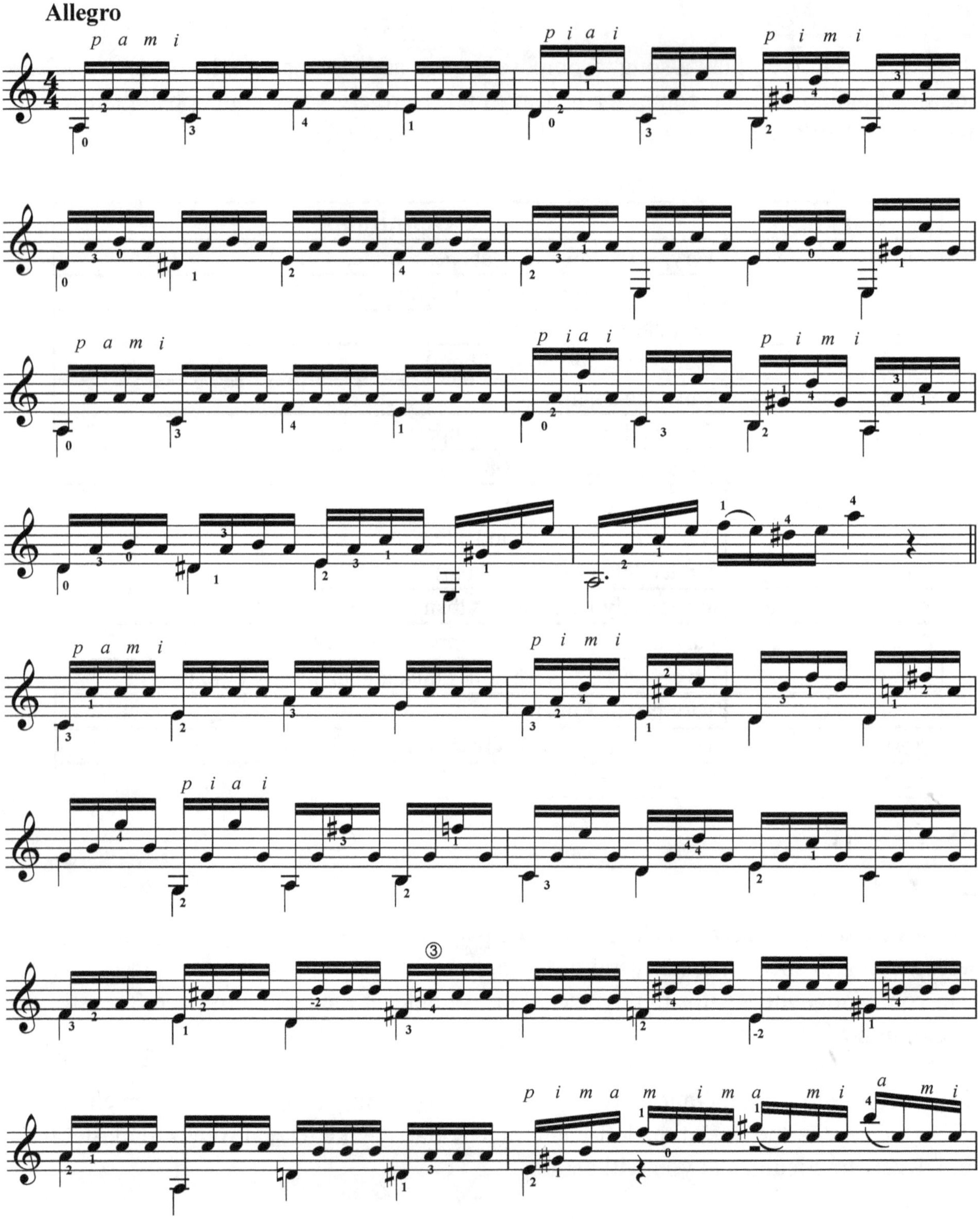

Etude in A - Remarks

In the next lessons, 'Etude in A' by Carcassi, the notes are in triplets. Triplets are counted 1&a 2&a, etc. On the 2nd measure, it's easier to slide your 2nd finger up a fret and use it as a guide, rather than taking all your fingers off the fretboard.

There are accent marks, the little 'greater than' sign, on beats 2 and 3. This means to play those notes louder than the rest. At the end of this first half, do you see the double bar with two dots? That is a repeat sign. You look for a similar double bar with two dots at the right of the bars. If you don't see that, you repeat to the beginning of the song. This one repeats to the beginning of the song.

LESSON 16

Etude in A

Etude in A

Matteo Carcassi

Read the remarks at the end of lesson 15, about the triplets, accents and repeats. Towards the end of the piece, there is a 'fermata' on the second to the last system on high 'D'. A fermata, or birds eye, means to pause for a moment on that note. Then it goes right back into the normal tempo.

This is the fermata: 𝄐

Aim for placing the as many fingers down at the same time as you can. It helps to relax your fingers in the middle of each change. Like the last song, this one may take a few weeks to master. Be patient and keep playing.

More Music Symbols

Here are other common musical terms you need to know.

Name	Meaning
D.C. or da capo	Jump to the 'Head' or beginning. Capo means Head in Italian.
D.S. or dal segno	Jump To the Sign
D.S al Coda	Jump to the sign until you see the to Coda, then jump to the Coda.
D.S al Fine	Jump to the sign and stop when you see Fine.
al Fine	Where the song ends. It may be in the middle of the music.
𝄋	The Sign, segno.
To Coda 𝄌	Jump to the Coda
𝄌 Coda	The Coda - The coda is the final section or passage of a piece.

Dynamics

Dynamic indications in music show how to play a section of music. Here are the dynamics you may see in music.

Name	Meaning
ppp	Pianississimo - Extremely soft. This is usually the softest indication used, but it can be softer with additional p's.
pp	Pianissimo - Very soft. This one is usually the softest indication in a piece of music.
p	Piano - Soft. Usually the most often used indication.
mf	Mezzo piano It literally means half as soft as piano.
mf	Mezzo forte - Half as loud as forte. If no dynamic appears, mezzo-forte is assumed to be the dynamic level..
f	Forte Loud. Used as often as piano to indicate contrast..
ff	Fortissimo - Very loud. Usually the loudest indication in a piece, though louder dynamics are often specified with additional f's.
fff	Fortississimo - Extremely loud. Usually the loudest indication used, but there are other with added f's.

Name	Meaning
sfz	Sforzando - Literally "forced", it is an abrupt, fierce accent on a single sound or chord. When written out in full, it applies to the sequence of sounds or chords under or over which it is placed.
fp	Forte-piano - A section of music in which the music should be played loudly (forte), then immediately softly (piano).
—	Crescendo - A gradual increase in volume. It can be extended under many notes to indicate that the volume steadily increases during the passage.
—	Diminuendo - Also decrescendo, a gradual decrease in volume. Can be extended under longer phrases.

Originally the piano was called Piano-Forte because it could play both soft and loud, unlike the other keyboard instruments that were plucked, like the harpsichord. I find it interesting that the name was changed to just Piano, which means 'soft'.

Where To Go From Here

I hope this book has been helpful for you. If you would like to see some of these lessons in DVD format, visit ReadingMusicOnYourGuitar.com. In addition, some of them are in our Music Theory Course. It begins similar to this book, but three quarters of the material is on music theory and how to apply it for writing and arranging your own songs.

Check out the resources at the end of this book. We have other courses specifically around topics like Mastering Finger Picking and more.

Join Our Newsletter Family

You may also want to join our Newsletter family. You will receive many guitar playing tips, free video lessons, and it is an excellent way to keep informed of other upcoming courses and resources. You can find that at our web site, WorshipGuitarClass.com or send an e-mail to subscribe@worshipguitarclass.com.

Jean Welles' Music Theory Course

Learn to read the notes on the guitar and learn all about music theory. Learn how different types of chords are constructed, and what chords fit in various keys. Discover different types of scales. Learn the Circle of Fifths and how to recognize any key.

Find out how to write songs and 35 ways to change and enhance what you have written. Learn how to transition or modulate into any key. There are hundreds, if not, thousands, of ways to write and arrange songs.

In the course, you will see many arrangements of songs with ideas of how to use the concepts for your own music. The course comes with two DVD's, over 5 1/2 hours of lessons that compliment the book.

It covers some of the material in this *Jean Welles' Music Reading On Your Guitar* book, but then includes the teaching videos and much more material about music theory and song arrangements.

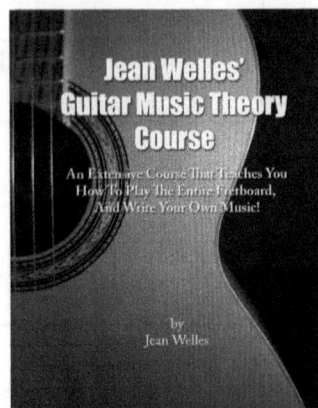

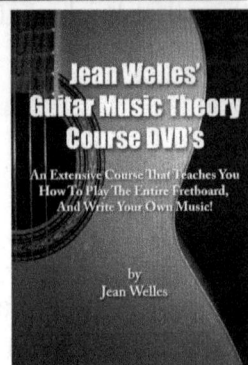

Jean Welles Worship Guitar Class™

With the 'Jean Welles Worship Guitar Class™' DVDs you will learn to play 28 worship songs. With the four volumes, you will learn how to play 60 chords and around 30 new strumming and finger picking patterns.

» Easy step-by-step lessons to help you understand and play each song.
» Booklets are included, in English and Spanish, in the DVD boxes which clearly show you all the songs, chords, and strumming patterns.
» Optional full size books are available, which include the musical notation of each song and are perfect for personal or classroom use.
» Learn to play popular worship songs for today and all times.
» A perfect gift for friends, adults, and kids age 10 and up.
» An excellent learning program for Christian homeschool kids age 10 and up.

'Jean Welles Worship Guitar Class™' for Kids

This worship guitar class program for kids will not only teach your child how to play the guitar, but it will reinforce Christian values. The lessons start with one-finger chord worship songs and plucking out melodies with individual fingers. Here is what your child, or children, will learn.

In this book and DVD course your child will learn:

» How to hold down a note to get a clear tone on the guitar.
» First 3 lessons use one-finger chords and melodies to help strengthen their fingers.
» Full chords introduced on lesson four.
» 9 guitar lessons with a 2 1/2 hour teaching DVD.
» Great for ages 5 - 9 and filmed with a 7 year old.
» Opens and closes with puppets skits and includes a gospel invitation at the end.

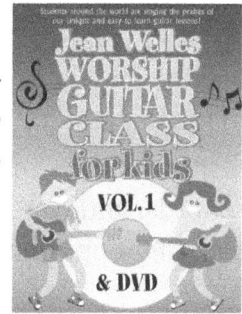

Jean Welles Worship Guitar Class™ - Mastering Finger Picking

In this Finger Picking course you will learn finger picking exercises, song accompaniments, and instrumental solos to expand your skills. All of the material in this book and DVD is new and not in the original Worship Guitar Class program.

* Finger Picking Exercises.
* A few Christmas songs to sing.
* Instrumental Solos.
* Songs with the Travis Pick.
* An hour of teaching in the DVD (12 Lessons).
* A book with the music and tips on playing.
* A Flamenco solo with the tremolo, rasqueado, and the tambour.

Jean Welles Worship Guitar Class™ - Christmas Songs and Solos.

This book and DVD is an excellent addition because it contains 14 solo arrangements of Christmas songs. The musical notation, guitar tab, chords, and words are included for each song. This book gives you more reading opportunities and is perfect for the Christmas season.

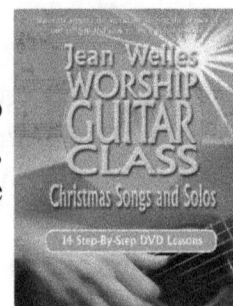

The Christmas Songs include:

1. What Child Is This
2. Deck The Halls
3. I Saw Three Ships
4. O Come All Ye Faithful
5. We Three Kings
6. Joy To The World
7. Hark The Herald Angels Sing
8. Angels We Have Heard On High
9. Go Tell It On The Mountain
10. God Rest Ye Merry Gentlemen
11. O Come, O Come, Emmanuel
12. Silent Night
13. O Little Town Of Bethlehem
14. O Holy Night

View Sample Videos - WorshipGuitarClass.com

Visit WorshipGuitarClass.com to view sample lessons from most of our courses, and view the list of stores that carry our courses. Plus, there are several free video lessons at the website. You can also sign up to become part of our Newsletter family at the website, or by sending an e-mail to: subscribe@worshipguitarclass.com.